In His Steps

Good Friday Ecumenical Worship Service

By Steven Bomely

In His Steps

Good Friday Ecumenical Worship Service

By Steven Bomely

C.S.S. Publishing Company, Inc.
Lima, Ohio

IN HIS STEPS: THE STATIONS OF THE CROSS

9119 / ISBN 1-55673-286-4   PRINTED IN U.S.A.

INTRODUCTION

I am convinced of the value of learning from various Christian traditions. I appreciate the richness of traditions other than my own. The Presbyterian Church (U.S.A.), Book of Order affirms this ecumenical approach; noting that the order of public worship should take into account and utilize "the historical experiences of the universal church that continues to be relevant and that are consistent with a right demonstration of the gospel." In applying this principle, "In His Steps" is a Protestant version of the "Stations of the Cross" experienced by Roman Catholics.

"In His Steps" is based on a program titled **"In His Steps" — Meditations on the last night and day in the life of our Lord and Savior, Jesus Christ,** by Dr. Mark A. Bayert, pastor of First Presbyterian Church, Bismarck, North Dakota. Dr. Bayert's program was designed for individual prayer and meditation as a supplement — not replacement — for corporate worship on Maundy Thursday and/or Good Friday. The stations were set up around the sanctuary, each station consisting of a chair or stand with the appropriate number and symbol — basin and towel, chalice, bag of coins, et cetera. In each case the worshiper sat in a pew closest to the station and silently read the suggested scripture and prayer before moving onto the next station. The stations were set up all day Good Friday — people could go through the stations anytime from 7 a.m. to 6 p.m. I am indebted to him for this program.

I adapted the original program for use in a public ecumenical Good Friday worship service. For each station, a person (different people could be used for each station) stood in a position clearly visible to the congregation holding up the appropriate symbol for that station and the leader announced the name of the station and the symbol for it; the scripture was read by one of the participants; and time was allowed for people to pray the printed prayer and meditate briefly.

One final suggestion might be made for the use of this service. Pastors should not feel bound by this service. Changes may be made to suit particular situations and other hymns may be substituted.

Grateful acknowledgment is made to Dr. Mark Bayert for permission to use his original program of "In His Steps" in this work.

Welcome

THE STATIONS OF THE CROSS

CALL TO WORSHIP

LEADER: Fear and fascination drew observers to the first Holy Friday. These emotions have attracted people ever since.

PEOPLE: We cannot flee from the pain and suffering which Jesus experienced on our behalf.

LEADER: We wonder why one so faithful and loving had to face the agony of rejection and death.

PEOPLE: Jesus was wounded for our transgressions, and was bruised for our sins.

LEADER: In this time of worship we join Christ at Calvary, aware of our involvement in the cruelty there.

PEOPLE: Our faithfulness is tested at the cross and our lives are judged by our response.

*HYMN "In the Cross of Christ I Glory"

Station 1

JESUS WASHES HIS DISCIPLE'S FEET

SYMBOL: Basin and Towel

SCRIPTURE: John 13:1-9

[1]It was just before the Passover feast. Jesus knew that the time had come for him to leave this world and go to the Father. Having loved his own who were in the world, he now showed them the full extent of his love. [2]The evening meal was being served, and the devil had already prompted Judas Iscariot, son of Simon, to betray Jesus. [3]Jesus knew that the Father had put all things under his power, and that he had come from God and was returning to God; [4]so he got up from the meal, took off his outer clothing, and wrapped a towel around his waist. [5]After that, he poured water into a basin and began to wash his disciples' feet, drying them with the towel that was wrapped around him. [6]He came to Simon Peter, who said to him, "Lord, are you going to wash my feet?" [7]Jesus replied, "You do not realize now what I am doing, but later you will understand." [8]"No," said Peter, "you shall never wash my feet." Jesus answered, "Unless I wash you, you have no part with me." [9]"Then, Lord," Simon Peter replied, "not just my feet but my hands and my head as well!"

SILENT PRAYERS: Lord God, we thank you for your Son's example of humility. He came to serve others, instead of bossing them around. Help us to be willing to wait on the needs of others and, at the same time, not be too proud to receive gestures of kindness, for Jesus' sake. Amen.

Station 2
JESUS EATS HIS LAST MEAL WITH THE DISCIPLES

SYMBOL: Chalice

SCRIPTURE: Matthew 26:26-29

[26]While they were eating, Jesus took bread, gave thanks and broke it, and gave it to his disciples, saying, "Take and eat; this is my body." [27]Then he took the cup, gave thanks and offered it to them, saying, "Drink from it, all of you. [28]This is my blood of the covenant, which is poured out for many for the forgiveness of sins. [29]I tell you, I will not drink of this fruit of the vine from now on until that day when I drink it anew with you in my Father's kingdom."

SILENT PRAYERS: God, all too innocently the disciples share that last supper with their Master. They didn't really appreciate what was about to happen. Jesus' puzzling words about his body and blood went over their heads. Yet in the end that communion would cost them their lives: with two exceptions, they would all become martyrs. Before we sit at the table with Christ, help us to weigh the cost of discipleship. Amen.

Station 3
JESUS PRAYS IN THE GARDEN

SYMBOL: Praying Hands

SCRIPTURE: Matthew 26:36-46

[36]Then Jesus went with his disciples to a place called Gethsemane, and he said to them, "Sit here while I go over there and pray." [37]He took Peter and the two sons of Zebedee along with him, and he began to be sorrowful and troubled. [38]Then he said to them, "My soul is overwhelmed with sorrow to the point of death. Stay here and keep watch with me." [39]Going a little farther, he fell with his face to the ground and prayed, "My Father, if it is possible, may this cup be taken from me. Yet not as I will, but as you will." [40]Then he returned to his disciples and found them sleeping. "Could you men not keep watch with me for one hour?" he asked Peter. [41]"Watch and pray so that you will not fall into temptation. The spirit is willing, but the body is weak." [42]He went away a second time and prayed, "My Father, if it is not possible for this cup to be taken away unless I drink it, may your will be done." [43]When he came back, he again found them sleeping, because their eyes were heavy. [44]So he left them and went away once more and prayed the third time, saying the same thing. [45]Then he returned to the disciples and said to them, "Are you still sleeping and resting? Look, the hour is near, and the Son of Man is betrayed into the hands of sinners. [46]Rise, let us go! Here comes my betrayer!"

SILENT PRAYERS: Heavenly Father, we remember Jesus' agony in Gethesemane. As he struggled with his destiny, he cried out to you in prayer. Help us also to turn to you in our times of need, to express our doubts and fears openly, and to be willing to accept your will for our lives. Amen.

*HYMN "Go to Dark Gethsemane"

Station 4
JESUS IS BETRAYED

SYMBOL: Bag of Coins

SCRIPTURE: Matthew 26:14-16, 47-49

[14]**Then one of the Twelve — the one called Judas Iscariot — went to the chief priests** [15]**and asked, "What are you willing to give me if I hand him over to you?" So they counted out for him thirty silver coins.** [16]**From then on Judas watched for an opportunity to hand him over.**

[47]**While he was still speaking, Judas, one of the Twelve, arrived. With him was a large crowd armed with swords and clubs, sent from the chief priests and the elders of the people.** [48]**Now the betrayer had arranged a signal with them: "The one I kiss is the man; arrest him."** [49]**Going at once to Jesus, Judas said, "Greetings, Rabbi!" and kissed him.**

SILENT PRAYERS: Lord, how it must have hurt Jesus that a close associate and friend turned out to be a traitor. Keep our faith steady so that our doubts don't turn to disillusionment. Help us not sell our souls for monetary gain. Amen.

Station 5
JESUS IS ARRESTED

SYMBOL: Rope

SCRIPTURE: Matthew 26:50-56

[50]Jesus replied, "Friend, do what you came for." Then the men stepped forward, seized Jesus and arrested him. [51]With that, one of Jesus' companions reached for his sword, drew it out and struck the servant of the high priest, cutting off his ear. [52]"Put your sword back in its place," Jesus said to him, "for all who draw the sword will die by the sword. [53]Do you think I cannot call on my Father, and he will at once put at my disposal more than twelve legions of angels? [54]But how then would the Scriptures be fulfilled that say it must happen in this way?" [55]At that time Jesus said to the crowd, "Am I leading a rebellion, that you have come out with swords and clubs to capture me? Every day I sat in the temple courts teaching, and you did not arrest me. [56]But this has all taken place that the writings of the prophets might be fulfilled." Then all the disciples deserted him and fled.

SILENT PRAYERS: God, when the secret police came in the night and laid their rough hands on Jesus, it was the beginning of the end. But he was so calm through it all. Help us to place our trust in you when our lives are interrupted by danger. Amen.

Station 6

JESUS IS DENIED

SYMBOL: Rooster

SCRIPTURE: Matthew 26:30-35

[30]When they had sung a hymn, they went out to the Mount of Olives. [31]Then Jesus told them, "This very night you will all fall away on account of men, for it is written: 'I will strike the shepherd, and the sheep of the flock will be scattered.' [32]But after I have risen, I will go ahead of you into Galilee." [33]Peter replied, "Even if all fall away on account of you, I never will." [34]"I tell you the truth," Jesus answered, "this very night, before the rooster crows, you will disown me three times." [35]But Peter declared, "Even if I have to die with you, I will never disown you." And all the other disciples said the same.

SCRIPTURE: Luke 22:54-62

[54]Then seizing him, they led him away and took him into the house of the high priest. Peter followed at a distance. [55]But when they had kindled a fire in the middle of the courtyard and had sat down together, Peter sat down with them. [56]A servant girl saw him seated there in the firelight. She looked closely at him and said, "This man was with him." [57]But he denied it. "Woman, I don't know him," he said. [58]A little later someone else saw him and said, "You also are one of them." "Man, I am not!" Peter replied. [59]About an hour later another asserted, "Certainly this fellow was with him, for he is a Galilean." [60]Peter replied, "Man, I don't know what you're

talking about!" Just as he was speaking, the rooster crowed. [61]The Lord turned and looked straight at Peter. Then Peter remembered the word the Lord had spoken to him: "Before the rooster crows today, you will disown me three times." [62]And he went outside and wept bitterly."

SILENT PRAYERS: Lord, Peter meant well. He followed Jesus to the judgment hall. But when the test came, he failed. Forgive you for the many ways in which we have let you down, for the many times we didn't have courage to stand up for what is right. Amen.

Station 7
JESUS IS CONDEMNED

SYMBOL: Gavel

SCRIPTURE: Mark 15:1-15

[1]Very early in the morning, the chief priests, with the elders, the teachers of the law and the whole Sanhedrin, reached a decision. They bound Jesus, led him away and handed him over to Pilate. [2]"Are you the king of the Jews?" asked Pilate. "Yes, it is as you say," Jesus replied. [3]The chief priests accused him of many things. [4]So again Pilate asked him, "Aren't you going to answer? See how many things they are accusing you of." [5]But Jesus still made no reply, and Pilate was amazed. [6]Now it was the custom at the Feast to release a prisoner whom the people requested. [7]A man called Barabbas was in prison with the insurrectionists who had committed murder in the uprising. [8]The crowd came up and asked Pilate to do for them what he usually did. [9]"Do you want me to release to you the king of the Jews?" asked Pilate, [10]knowing it was out of envy that the chief priests had handed Jesus over to him. [11]But the chief priests stirred up the crowd to have Pilate release Barabbas instead. [12]"What shall I do, then, with the one you call the king of the Jews?" Pilate asked them. [13]"Crucify him!" they shouted. [14]"Why? What crime has he committed?" asked Pilate. But they shouted all the louder, "Crucify him!" [15]Wanting to satisfy the crowd, Pilate released Barabbas to them. He had Jesus flogged, and handed him over to be crucified.

SILENT PRAYERS: They called that a trial, Lord. Trumped up charges, a judge who gave in to the demands of a mob — what injustice! We live in a world where the guilty get away with murder and the innocent senselessly suffer. We pray today for all victims of injustice. Amen.

SPECIAL MUSIC

Station 8
JESUS IS MOCKED

SYMBOL: Crown of Thorns

SCRIPTURE: Mark 15:16-20

[16]The soldiers led Jesus away into the palace (that is, the Praetorium) and called together the whole company of soldiers. [17]They put a purple robe on him, then twisted together a crown of thorns and set it on him. [18]And they began to call out to him, "Hail, king of the Jews!" [19]Again and again they struck him on the head with a staff and spit on him. Falling on their knees, they paid homage to him. [20]And when they had mocked him, they took off the purple robe and put his own clothes on him. Then they led him out to crucify him.

SILENT PRAYERS: Holy God, is there anything more cruel than a bunch of bullies ganging up on a helpless victim. A crown of thorns — what a sick joke, what perverted humor! Forgive us for the times we have stood silently at the edge of a crowd or actively joined in when someone different from or weaker than us was being belittled and humiliated. Have mercy. Amen.

Station 9
JESUS CARRIES HIS CROSS

SYMBOL: Chunk of Wood

SCRIPTURE: Luke 23:26-32

[26]As they led him away, they seized Simon from Cyrene, who was on his way in from the country, and put the cross on him and made him carry it behind Jesus. [27]A large number of people followed him, including women who mourned and wailed for him. [28]Jesus turned and said to them, "Daughters of Jerusalem, do not weep for me; weep for yourselves and for your children. [29]For the time will come when you will say, 'Blessed are the barren women, the wombs that never bore and the breasts that never nursed!' [30]Then 'they will say to the mountains, "Fall on us!" and to the hills, "Cover us!" ' [31]For if men do these things when the tree is green, what will happen when it is dry?" [32]Two other men, both criminals, were also led out with him to be executed.

SILENT PRAYERS: Father, it must have felt like Jesus was carrying the weight of the whole world on his shoulders. It was too much. He collapsed. We can picture him with tears in our eyes — God lying bruised and bleeding in the dust. We remember how they forced a stranger to carry the cross for him. Help us to step forth willingly to shoulder the burden of others. Amen.

JESUS IS NAILED TO THE CROSS

SYMBOL: Nails

SCRIPTURE: Luke 23:33-43

[33]When they came to the place called the Skull, there they crucifed him, along with the criminals — one on his right, the other on his left. [34]Jesus said, "Father, forgive them, for they do not know what they are doing." And they divided up his clothes by casting lots. [35]The people stood watching, and the rulers even sneered at him. They said, "He saved others; let him save himself if he is the Christ of God, the Chosen One." [36]The soldiers also came up and mocked him. They offered him wine vinegar [37]and said, "If you are the king of the Jews, save yourself." [38]There was a written notice above him, which read: THIS IS THE KING OF THE JEWS. [39]One of the criminals who hung there hurled insults at him: "Aren't you the Christ? Save yourself and us!" [40]But the other criminal rebuked him. "Don't you fear God," he said, "since you are under the same sentence? [41]We are punished justly, for we are getting what our deeds deserve. But this man has done nothing wrong." [42]Then he said, "Jesus, remember me when you come into your kingdom." [43]Jesus answered him, "I tell you the truth, today you will be with me in paradise."

SILENT PRAYERS: Lord, what pain Jesus endured — all for us! Yet he had the presence of mind — and the unbelievable selflessness — to forgive his executioners and to welcome the contrite thief to paradise. Grant us grace to be able to forgive our enemies. Amen.

JESUS DIES ON THE CROSS

SYMBOL: Death Certificate

SCRIPTURE: Mark 15:33-39

[33]At the sixth hour darkness came over the whole land until the ninth hour. [34]And at the ninth hour Jesus cried out in a loud voice, "Eloi, Eloi, lama sabachthani?" — which means "My God, my God, why have you forsaken me?" [35]When some of those standing near heard this, they said, "Listen, he's calling Elijah." [36]One man ran, filled a sponge with wine vinegar, put it on a stick, and offered it to Jesus to drink. "Now leave him alone. Let's see if Elijah comes to take him down," he said. [37]With a loud cry, Jesus breathed his last. [38]The curtain of the temple was torn in two from top to bottom. [39]And when the centurion, who stood there in front of Jesus, heard his cry and saw how he died, he said, "Surely this man was the Son of God!"

SILENT PRAYERS: It was all over for him, Lord. Our Savior gasped for his last breath and released a final agonizing cry, feeling deserted not only by his friends but even by you. Help us to appreciate more than ever before the sacrifice of the Lamb of God for our salvation. Amen.

MEDITATION

Station 12
JESUS IS BURIED

SYMBOL: Shovel

SCRIPTURE: Mark 15:40-47

[40]Some women were watching from a distance. Among them were Mary Magdalene, Mary the mother of James the younger and of Joses, and Salome. [41]In Galilee these women had followed him and cared for his needs. Many other women who had come up with him to Jerusalem were also there. [42]It was Preparation Day (that is, the day before the Sabbath). So as evening approached, [43]Joseph of Arimathea, a prominent member of the Council, who was himself waiting for the kingdom of God, went boldly to Pilate and asked for Jesus' body. [44]Pilate was surprised to hear that he was already dead. Summoning the centurion, he asked him if Jesus had already died. [45]When he learned from the centurion that it was so, he gave the body to Joseph. [46]So Joseph brought some linen cloth, took down the body, wrapped it in the linen, and placed it in a tomb cut out of rock. Then he rolled a stone against the entrance of the tomb. [47]Mary Magdalene and Mary the mother of Joses saw where he was laid.

SILENT PRAYERS: God, those faithful women were stunned and speechless as they laid Jesus in the tomb. All their hopes were buried with him. You assured us in the darkest hours of our lives that our saving purpose will not be defeated — that death will be followed by resurrection, that good will triumph over evil. In the name of him who was dead but is risen. Amen.

*HYMN "O Sacred Head, Now Wounded"

OFFERING

*DOXOLOGY AND DEDICATION

LORD'S PRAYER

*HYMN "When I Survey the Wondrous Cross"

*CLOSING RESPONSE

LEADER: Go out to keep your vigil at the cross. Let prayer and meditation be a means of transformation.

PEOPLE: We carry with us the tragedy of this day. But also its possibilities for reclaiming a heritage and recovering a faith to sustain and move us.

LEADER: Share the agony of Jesus' rejection and death, knowing how often we add to the pain.

PEOPLE: Our intent is to take up our cross and follow. But we shrink from the anguish and falter at the cost.

LEADER: Say "yes" to the Christ, without excuses or reservations.

PEOPLE: Worthy is the One who was slain, to receive the glory and honor, and power.

*BENEDICTION

In His Steps

Good Friday Ecumenical Worship
Suggested Order of Service For Bulletin

GOOD FRIDAY ECUMENICAL WORSHIP
For Use As A Church Bulletin

WELCOME

CALL TO WORSHIP

LEADER: Fear and fascination drew observers to the first Holy Friday. These emotions have attracted people ever since.
PEOPLE: We cannot flee from the pain and suffering which Jesus experienced on our behalf.
LEADER: We wonder why one so faithful and loving had to face the agony of rejection and death.
PEOPLE: Jesus was wounded for our transgressions, and was bruised for our sins.
LEADER: In this time of worship we join Christ at Calvary, aware of our involvement in the cruelty there.
PEOPLE: Our faithfulness is tested at the cross and our lives are judged by our response.

*HYMN "In the Cross of Christ I Glory"

STATIONS OF THE CROSS

1. **JESUS WASHES HIS DISCIPLE'S FEET**
   SYMBOL — Basin and Towel
   SCRIPTURE: John 13:1-9

SILENT PRAYERS: Lord God, we thank you for your Son's example of humility. He came to serve others, instead of bossing them around. Help us to be willing to wait on the needs of others and, at the same time, not be too proud to receive gestures of kindness, for Jesus' sake. Amen.

2. **JESUS EATS HIS LAST MEAL WITH THE DISCIPLES**
   SYMBOL — Chalice
   SCRIPTURE: Matthew 26:26-29
   SILENT PRAYERS: God, all too innocently the disciples share that last supper with their Master. They didn't really appreciate what was about to happen. Jesus' puzzling words about his body and blood went over their heads. Yet in the end that communion would cost them their lives: with two exceptions, they would all become martyrs. Before we sit at the table with Christ, help us to weigh the cost of discipleship. Amen.

3. **JESUS PRAYS IN THE GARDEN**
   SYMBOL — Praying Hands
   SCRIPTURE: Matthew 26:36-46
   SILENT PRAYERS: Heavenly Father, we remember Jesus' agony in Gethsemane. As he struggled with his destiny, he cried out to you in prayer. Help us also to turn to you in our times of need, to express our doubts and fears openly, and to be willing to accept your will for our lives. Amen.

*HYMN "Go to Dark Gethsemane"

4. **JESUS IS BETRAYED**
   SYMBOL — Bag of Coins
   SCRIPTURE: Matthew 26:14-16, 47-49
   SILENT PRAYERS: Lord, how it must have hurt Jesus that a close associate and friend turned out to

be a traitor. Keep our faith steady so that our doubts don't turn to disillusionment. Help us not sell our souls for monetary gain. Amen.

5. JESUS IS ARRESTED
SYMBOL — Rope
SCRIPTURE: Matthew 26:50-56
SILENT PRAYERS: God, when the secret police came in the night and laid their rough hands on Jesus, it was the beginning of the end. But he was so calm through it all. Help us to place our trust in you when our lives are interrupted by danger. Amen.

6. JESUS IS DENIED
SYMBOL — Rooster
SCRIPTURE: Luke 22:54-62
Matthew 26:30-35
SILENT PRAYERS: Lord, Peter meant well. He followed Jesus to the judgment hall. But when the test came, he failed. Forgive us for the many ways in which we have let you down, for the many times we didn't have courage to stand up for what is right. Amen.

7. JESUS IS CONDEMNED
SYMBOL — Gavel
SCRIPTURE: Mark 15:1-15
SILENT PRAYERS: They called that a trial, Lord. Trumped up charges, a judge who gave in to the demands of a mob — what injustice! We live in a world where the guilty get away with murder and the innocent senselessly suffer. We pray today for all victims of injustice. Amen.

SPECIAL MUSIC

8. JESUS IS MOCKED

SYMBOL — Crown of Thorns

SCRIPTURE: Mark 15:16-20

SILENT PRAYERS: Holy God, is there anything more cruel than a bunch of bullies ganging up on a helpless victim. A crown of thorns — what a sick joke, what perverted humor! Forgive us for the times we have stood silently at the edge of a crowd or actively joined in when someone different from or weaker than us was being belittled and humiliated. Have mercy. Amen.

9. JESUS CARRIES HIS CROSS

SYMBOL — Chunk of Wood

SCRIPTURE: Luke 23:26-32

SILENT PRAYERS: Father, it must have felt like Jesus was carrying the weight of the whole world on his shoulders. It was too much. He collapsed. We can picture him with tears in our eyes — God lying bruised and bleeding in the dust. We remember how they forced a stranger to carry the cross for him. Help us to step forth willingly to shoulder the burder of others. Amen.

10. JESUS IS NAILED TO THE CROSS

SYMBOL — Nails

SCRIPTURE: Luke 23:33-43

SILENT PRAYERS: Lord, what pain Jesus endured — all for us! Yet he had the presence of mind — and the unbelievable selflessness — to forgive his executioners and to welcome the contrite thief to paradise. Grant us grace to be able to forgive our enemies. Amen.

11. JESUS DIES ON THE CROSS

SYMBOL — Death Certificate

SCRIPTURE: Mark 15:33-39

SILENT PRAYERS: It was all over for him, Lord. Our Savior gasped for his last breath and released a final agonizing cry, feeling deserted not only by his friends but even by you. Help us to appreciate more than ever before the sacrifice of the Lamb of God for our salvation. Amen.

MEDITATION

12. JESUS IS BURIED
SYMBOL — Shovel
SCRIPTURE: Mark 15:40-47
SILENT PRAYERS: God, those faithful women were stunned and speechless as they laid Jesus in the tomb. All their hopes were buried with him. You assured us in the darkest hours or our lives that our saving purpose will not be defeated that death will be followed by resurrection, that good will triumph over evil. In the name of him who was dead but is risen. Amen.

*HYMN "O Sacred Head, Now Wounded"

OFFERING

*DOXOLOGY and DEDICATION

LORD'S PRAYER

*HYMN "When I Survey the Wondrous Cross"

*CLOSING RESPONSE

LEADER: Go out to keep your vigil at the cross. Let prayer and meditation be a means of transformation.
PEOPLE: We carry with us the tragedy of this day. But also its possibilities for reclaiming a heritage and recovering a faith to sustain and move us.

LEADER: Share the agony of Jesus' rejection and death, knowing how often we add to the pain.

PEOPLE: Our intent is to take up our cross and follow. But we shrink from the anguish and falter at the cost.

LEADER: Say "yes" to the Christ, without excuses or reservations.

PEOPLE: Worthy is the One who was slain, to receive glory and honor, and power.

*BENEDICTION

www.ingramcontent.com/pod-product-compliance
Lightning Source LLC
Chambersburg PA
CBHW060044040426
42331CB00032B/2400